The Gentle Art of
Hospitality

ALDA ELLIS

Artwork by

CAMILLE ELLERBROOK

HARVEST HOUSE PUBLISHERS

EUGENE, OREGON

Interior design by Garborg Design Works, Savage, MN
Cover illustration by Garborg Design Works, Savage, MN

Artwork © Camille Ellerbrook. License Granted by Gifford B. Bowne II of Indigo Gate, Inc., One Pegasus Drive, Colts Neck, NJ 07722-1490, USA, Tel: (732) 577-9333, www.IndigoGate.com.

Harvest House Publishers has made every effort to trace the ownership of all poems and quotes. In the event of a question arising from the use of a poem or quote, we regret any error made and will be pleased to make the necessary correction in future editions of this book.

THE GENTLE ART OF HOSPITALITY

Copyright © 2007 Text by Alda Ellis; Artwork by Camille Ellerbrook, courtesy of
    Indigo Gate, Inc.
Published by Harvest House Publishers
Eugene, Oregon 97402

ISBN-13: 978-0-7369-2100-8
ISBN-10: 0-7369-2100-1

Printed in China

07 08 09 10 11 12 13 14 15 / LP / 10 9 8 7 6 5 4 3 2 1

Contents

The Gift of Time

In the midst of our busy schedules, it's easy to get caught up in the world's hectic pace. With high-speed, high-tech conveniences and modern innovations such as cell phones, commuter travel, fax machines, email, satellite dishes, and iPods, there is a need to celebrate the art of gracious living and the gift of hospitality.

Entertaining doesn't always have to mean putting on a lavish affair. It can also mean an offering of something to drink, to eat, and a gift of what is so precious to most of us—our time. I can offer a glass of sweet, iced tea to my husband as he comes in the door from work, or I can offer it warm in delicate china teacups to a group of 20 quite easily.

The spirit of graciousness was exemplified on a daily basis as I was growing up in a Southern home surrounded by strong Southern women. Even on a very modest budget, amid the sweet-smelling honeysuckle, gardenias, and magnolias, my mother, grandmother, and aunts extended generous doses of hospitality to all who crossed their thresholds. From their example, I learned how to set a proper table, sew a slipcover, bake a Red Velvet Cake, prune the rosebushes, and make great brewed, sweet, iced tea.

Did you notice that each of the five senses were involved? Each task rose above the mundane and took on an important meaning of caring for home and family. The heartfelt lesson is that hospitality is a gift of time that says welcome into our home, welcome into our day.

The way we love our families and friends is through the definition of gracious: "a generosity of spirit, characterized by kindness and warm courtesy" to those we live with and those who visit. That also means that we should decorate our homes not to impress people, but to offer a sense of sanctuary from the outside world and a place of peace for the souls of those who live and visit there.

> *Do not neglect to show hospitality to strangers, for by this some have entertained angels without knowing it.*
>
> HEBREWS 13:2

Style cannot be bought. It is not what you wear, but who you are. Style is the way you decorate your house. It is your taste in books, music, poetry, and art. It's the way you arrange your flowers. Style is the personal touch you give to everything and everyone in your life. Style has nothing to do with money, but it is the way you live your life.

ALDA

The way we mold our homes silently speaks volumes about us. Being in the Home Décor and Gift Industry, I've had the opportunity to visit many designer showrooms in New York, Dallas, Chicago, Los Angeles, and Atlanta. I have learned that the most important "style" isn't someone else's look. It's more important to fill a home with things that have meaning to the people who live there. What we select for the public and private areas of our homes—the table-tops, the bookshelves, the books, the mantels, and our bedside tables—reflect who we are.

My personal home has evolved in style over the last 25 years. Through the years I have come to appreciate a much simpler style. My furniture consists of family heirlooms mixed with special keep-sakes. The accessories are things we actually use, such as my grandmother's silver teapot. Baskets hold the little things, and a handmade quilt waiting to be used during a Sunday-afternoon nap is thrown over the ottoman. My style says that people actually "live here" instead of what is in vogue this month.

At the same time, I'm also known for creative entertaining on small and large scales. I've had countless guests who have expressed their appreciation for my home, my family, and my hospitality. A home that sends forth a generosity of spirit "characterized by kindness and indulgent courtesy," a home that welcomes both family and friends with heartfelt sincerity—that is what I strive for and what I share with you within the pages of this book. The warm nurturing of souls is the true gift of hospitality.

Blessings,

Alda Ellis

Hospitality
Begins at the Door

You never get a second chance to make a first impression.

WILL ROGERS

Entertaining with hospitality begins with inspiration, preparation, and presentation. Special occasions, and even some "made-up" reasons to celebrate, are the sources of my inspiration. The preparation can be simple or elaborate. With a single cup of tea or hosting a grand soiree, we're offering gracious hospitality that says, "Welcome! You are special." With the "Checklist of Senses" I present in this book, you'll feel more comfortable holding gatherings of 2 people or 200. From lighting to linens, from food to flowers, the ideas I share are simple, quick, and easy to do while entertaining from the heart.

Does entertaining seem too much for you? Are you concerned you don't have the space or the dishes or the wherewithal? I once attended a Christmas Tea that was hosted in a cozy room of a very small home. Everyone was asked to bring her own teacup and a friendship story to share. It was a delightful gathering, and one the participants remember with gladness more than 25 years later!

God asks us to offer hospitality without grumbling (1 Peter 4:9). A simple glass of water with a slice of lemon on the rim is a wonderful presentation if our hearts are in the right place.

My great-grandmother used to share how difficult times were and how hard the day-to-day living was during the Civil War. There was no tea to drink, and certainly no lemons for lemonade, which was a favorite Southern drink. However, she set a fine example of gracious hospitality even then. When guests came, she would go to the well or to the spring and fetch cold water. She served this refreshment in her grand silver Tea Tipper, an ornate teapot that sat in a cradle and could be tipped to pour the liquid into a cup. The cup she offered her guest was the one *without* the chip on the rim. Grandma never lost her sense of giving.

The spirit of gracious hospitality lives in each of us regardless of our circumstances. The ambience we create for our guests is warm, genuine hospitality... not based on what we have or what we can buy. My sister and I grew up with very little money, but we didn't know that until we were grown and realized what a wonderful home our mother had created out of very little. Her wit and wisdom gave us a wonderful foundation to build our lives and homes on.

With a cup of inspiration, a slice of determination, a pinch of humility, and a generous helping of hospitality, we found that anything is possible. With these ingredients poured into a bowl, we could stir up friendships and family relationships to last a lifetime.

Presentation, meaning our heart attitude, is crucial, for that is the great commandment: "And to love Him with all the heart, with all the understanding, with all the soul, and with all the strength, and to love one's neighbor as oneself, is more than all the whole burnt offerings and sacrifices" (Mark 12:33 NKJV). Through hospitality we do as God has asked us to do: present the love of Christ.

If you don't think your room is big enough to have a tea or party, consider hosting the party outdoors. By just being in an outdoor setting, food seems to taste better!

INNOVATIVE IDEAS TO PERSONALIZE YOUR HOME

My husband and I live in a turn-of-the-century home. Before we moved in, our house was vacant for a few years and begged for someone to lovingly care for it. It took months for the renovation, but those driving by could see the changes as our place became a home again.

For appearance, we added our street number to our front gate. The shiny brass numbers were visible from a distance and neatly marked our address. Clearly marking our street address and making it easy to be seen from a distance was a practical and decorative consideration. Experiment with ideas that suit your own style of house. Make sure that the numbers are easy to read from the street or, if on an apartment, easy to identify.

Once your guests have found the right address, it is nice to direct them toward the door you want them to use. Our house has five outside doors, but only one I want my guests to come to. I let friends and strangers alike know which door to use by having a walkway anchored by an urn of cascading blossoms. Flowers greeting a guest are a sign of welcome. Another idea is to direct your guests toward the door by a walkway strewn with hurricane lanterns during the nighttime or for a special evening event. Monkey grass lining the walkway will also direct guests on a daily basis.

Make sure the walkway porch and steps are swept clean and look cared for. As your guests walk up to your door, make them feel as though you have rolled out the red carpet for them. A clean entrance is a sure sign of a home lovingly cared for. Glass that sparkles, cobwebs kept away, and the absence of those pesky little spiders that love corners are telltale signs that the people who live

> *Every house where love abides, and friendship is a guest, is surely home—and home, sweet home—for there the heart can rest.*
>
> HENRY VAN DYKE

just beyond the door care about their home and environment.

A clean, attractive doormat makes for a good first impression. In the spirit of "bringing the indoors out, and the outdoors in," I sometimes purchase a small, inexpensive, Oriental-style rug to use as an outside mat for a bit of a change. It softens the line between the two worlds.

After dark, a gas-lit lamp can keep the entrance easy to see and safe.

"COME ON IN"

Sometimes God uses ordinary people with a simple message so others may come to know him. My mother never let the lack of money hold her back from inviting anyone into our home. Unexpected company was always offered the greeting, "Come on in." Mother even used to set up a humble little card table as an extension of our family's table when guests came so food could be offered and hearts nourished.

No matter how inadequate we may feel, God is still God, and he may be using us in some unknown way. The important thing is to reach out to others.

The most beautiful things in the world cannot be seen or even touched. They must be felt with the heart.

HELEN KELLER

A CHECKLIST OF THE SENSES

When I walk into a room and it "feels" good, I know I have thoroughly noted and considered what I call my "Checklist of the Senses." I reflect on my home and hope that my guests will feel welcome and comfortable, as in this delightful, welcoming description:

I think of half-past four at Manderlay, and the table drawn before the library fire...the performance, never varying, of...the silver tray, the kettle, the snowy cloth. (From *Rebecca,* by Daphne du Maurier.)

Rebecca is one of my all-time favorite classics. In this passage, she refers to "Afternoon Tea" by painting a picture with all the senses. You can hear the clock strike half-past four, taste the delicious tea, see the beautiful silver tray, smell the library fire, and touch the snowy cloth. All five senses have been firmly established. See, taste, hear, smell, and touch. This is a great hospitality secret!

Being aware of the five senses is always in the back of my mind. When guests enter a room in my home, I want them to see something attractive, such as noticing that the room is picked up from clutter. I'll offer them something to drink—such as a delightful glass of iced tea and something to eat, such as the delicious Pineapple Cookies I share below. *Taste* is such an easy sense to please. *Hearing* is addressed by a

> *Share your belongings with your needy fellow Christian, and open your homes to strangers.*
> ROMANS 12:13 GNT

pleasing sound in the background, which is not the television. Smells of freshly picked gardenias or scented candles burning fill the air. I tuck a little something into their hand—*touch*—when they leave…a recipe, a phone number, a flower picked from the garden. So simple, yes, but so touching and pleasing.

Friends and family will love these pineapple cookies that are simple yet so delicious!

PINEAPPLE COOKIES
(Yield: about 5 dozen cookies)

1 cup butter-flavor shortening
1½ cups sugar
1 egg
1 can (8¾ oz.) crushed pineapple, with juice

3½ cups flour
1 teaspoon baking soda
½ teaspoon salt
½ teaspoon nutmeg
½ cup chopped pecans

Heat oven to 400 degrees.

In a large bowl, mix shortening, sugar, and egg thoroughly. Stir in pineapple. Stir together flour (if you use self-rising flour omit the following baking soda and salt), baking soda, salt, and nutmeg. Blend well. Mix in nuts. Cover the bowl with plastic wrap and chill the dough for 1 hour.

Drop teaspoon-sized balls of dough about 2 inches apart on a parchment paper-lined baking sheet. (I use a Silpat.) Bake 8 minutes or until no imprint remains when touched lightly.

Checklist of the Senses
Sight

Martha was distracted with much serving....
But Mary has chosen that good part, which will not be taken away from her.
LUKE 10:40,42 NKJV

By keeping in mind the "Checklist of the Senses," we can create an ambience that leaves a lasting memory. A wonderful memory is a precious gift in itself to both family and friends and often tugs on our heart-strings. The special memory we want to create begins with the way we present ourselves on a daily basis to family, friends, and the occasional stranger. *Sight* is the first on my check-list. When entertaining, the look is important, but only how it relates to what is *really* important.

The story of offering hospitality is shared beautifully in the Bible when Mary and Martha are so excited over their honored guest, Jesus. Martha became so busy with all the preparations involved with preparing a meal for Jesus that she was more concerned with her work than she was with the *focus* of her hospitality—her guest. What she was doing became more important than her Lord. Mary, on the other hand, stopped her work and gave her full attention with a listening ear.

What we need to remember is that even as we delight our sense of sight, the most important things are to have our guests feel comfortable and welcome.

THE KITCHEN

The kitchen is often the heart of a home. When I am entertaining, it seems everyone wants to gather in my kitchen no matter where the party started. We can create a warm and welcoming atmosphere by how we decorate. Here are a few ideas so you'll always be prepared for expected…and unexpected…company.

First, display and use your beautiful things. Looking at what you've gathered together and collected is part of the enjoyment. But go a step further and use the things you love on the people you love. I am always amazed at the people who own beautiful china and silver yet have them packed away. Using beautiful treasures is part of the enjoyment!

Are you embarrassed because your silver is tarnished? Here are some great tips:

- The more you use silver, the richer the patina becomes.

- Make sure your silver is dry when putting it away.

- Keep chalk in the drawer to absorb moisture.

- Never use newspaper or rubber bands. The chemicals will damage the silver.

- Don't wear rubber gloves when polishing for the same reason.

- Use a silver cloth when storing. (Don't wash the silver cloth. It contains chemicals to keep the silver from oxidizing.)

Use the things you love on the people you love.
ALDA

When entertaining, a beautiful presentation adds to the taste. The chef at the Ritz Carlton once told me, "Presentation is everything, for we eat with our eyes." If it looks delicious, it will often taste more so. Sometimes the smallest details can add so much! Fresh strawberries in a stemmed goblet look much more attractive simply because of the way they are presented. Add a sprig of mint, a slice of lemon, a twisted slice of orange, or a sugarcoated violet as a tiny detail to a dessert, an entrée, or even to a dinner plate—and it will look like a million.

Here are some other fun kitchen hints:

- If you have mismatched chairs from an antique store, painting them all the same color will create a unified set.

- Transform any tablescape into a memorable moment with the addition of candlelight. Candlelight after sundown used to be the rule, but today candle-glow creates a warm atmosphere anytime.

- Anchor your table setting with beautiful flowers. A handful of roses from a garden fence placed in an antique milk bottle is quite charming. Or use a wooden bowl or urn full of bright green apples.

- Dishes don't have to match. Mix colors and shapes that coordinate well to create an interesting table.

- Tablecloths don't have to "fit" the table. If the table-cloth is too small, lay it at an angle with only the corners draping over the edge. Or a scrunched-up tablecloth in the center of the table gives a look of abundance.

- For festive events, tie corners of tablecloths with satin or velvet ribbons. If you want to tuck in flowers, a water tube from the florist will help nosegays of fresh flowers last longer.

The beautiful is as useful as the useful.
Perhaps more so.
VICTOR HUGO

• Remember, dishes and decorations don't have to be expensive. Pressed-glass ice tea glasses look wonderful indoors or out and create a gracious setting with formal or informal dishes.

• Mix gold and silver. It gives the table an "acquired over time" richness.

• Add dressy details. Flea-market finds, such as jewelry, can be mixed with heirloom silverware for stunning effects.

• Add height to your tables. Different heights are more pleasing to the eye and add interest.

• Use your indoor tableware out, and your outdoors in. A garden-themed tea might combine dining room silver with terra cotta saucers for plates. I recently lined a table with black plastic and topped it with woodland moss as a tablecloth. The reward for this table setting was the "Wow!" from my guests.

An attractively set table is a feast for the eyes as well as a perfect way to set a mood. On a day-to-day basis, use real dinner plates and real silverware or flatware when gathered around the dinner table. Sometimes with my schedule, I pick up "fast food." But still we set the table and

Serve one another in love.
GALATIANS 5:13 NIV

get the glasses filled with ice and tea. This prepares us for meeting around our table to share our joys, concerns, and blessings.

If you can't sit down together every day, make a point of eating together at least once a week. Put down the newspaper, magazine, and turn off the television. Share daily happenings with one another. Make eye contact. Set the mood by creating a family tradition of saying grace before meals.

Some people think the three basic food groups are canned, frozen, and take-out. At our house, weekends bring a bit more time for preparing "comfort food." Comfort food does not come through a drive-thru window! Slow down the pace with meatloaf and mashed potatoes, a Crock-Pot of homemade soup, or warm bread fresh out of the oven. The food tastes great! Seize the moments of interaction and meaningful dialog. The importance and focus is the gathering around the dinner table to share our daily lives.

CREATE A WARM KITCHEN WELCOME

- Eliminate counter clutter. Have a place where mail and other papers can accumulate, such as a wooden tray or basket.

- Have a teapot and two teacups on a tray ready for company.

- Have fun and unique items displayed. Search antique shops for vintage kitchen utensils and modern-day kitchen stores for the latest in tools.

- Use beautiful napkins. It's okay if they don't match.

- A chandelier adds formality to an eat-in kitchen. Embellish and personalize it with small lampshades. You can create cozy kitchen corners with little lamps.

- Displaying things from your family's past and present that are meaningful and cherished personalize a home. I use toys, books, and games from my childhood. A white porcelain door-knob is on our fireplace mantel. It was from the log cabin my father was born in.

- When you know someone is arriving, prop a small chalkboard on an easel in the foyer. Write his or her name on it and a brief note or thoughtful quote for a warm welcome. Use the slate for family members, too!

- Always have a vase of fresh flowers somewhere in the kitchen. To make them last longer, place them in the refrigerator at night.

- Keep fresh herbs such as cilantro, rosemary, parsley, or sage in bundles in a small vase of water in the refrig-erator. Trim the stems when you purchase the herbs, and they'll last twice as long. It adds a pretty touch when you open the door, too.

THE BACK DOOR

Most of my family and close friends enter through our back door, which is our mudroom. Even if it is the "back door," I am very aware of what they will see the minute they enter. To make this area inviting, I have an antique coatrack and boot tray there to catch the outerwear as it is peeled off. Umbrellas are standing tall in a vintage pickle crock. A large wooden bowl serves as a catch-all for the mail and papers brought home from school. A large, white platter catches my husband's car keys and pocket change when he comes home. A little silver teapot lamp is on the nearby table to offer a light of welcome. A cheerful "Come on in" called out from the nearby kitchen lets both friends and family know they are warmly welcomed.

EDIBLE FLOWER GARNISHES

Some of these flowers are quite pretty as they are, and others may be embellished with crystallizing. Simply brush the petals lightly with egg white. Over wax paper, sprinkle with superfine sugar. Let air dry, and store in an airtight container until used. Frosted pink rose petals and frosted purple grapes are so pretty together.

Calendula   Dandelion   Lavender   Marigold

Nasturtium   Pansy   Rose   Violet

An Entertaining
Note on Lighting

The lighting in a room creates atmosphere for dinner parties and family dinners. Assess the lighting in each room of your home. Natural lighting is always best. When we see well, we actually feel better.

I am a fan of dimmer switches for most rooms. A dimmer switch can be purchased at your local home-improvement store, and they are easy to install. Light can also be adjusted by using different wattages in light fixtures, but then you can't modify the lighting for different needs at different times.

Think about the four levels to lighting a room. One is the overall general lighting that lets us see our way into the room. In the evening, the light should be bright enough to see, but not harsh. Second is focused lighting that is used for certain tasks, such as reading or sewing. Down lit lamps are most effective for this. Third is ambience lighting. Ambience lighting is using small buffet lamps or table lamps to create cozy corners and an intimate feeling in the room. It also includes an elongated picture light to focus on a certain piece of artwork.

There's also decorative lighting. I love the mood of candlelight. I am always tucking votive candles in unexpected places for atmosphere. Remember to use little lamps in the kitchen as well as in the living room. It is thoughtful to have

small lamps in the bathroom that can be left on for your guests. You can count on the bathroom being used during a party, so it needs to reflect a festive atmosphere.

Since I love entertaining outdoors, lighting here is most important. Think of lighting your outdoor space on a daily basis differently than you do for outdoor entertaining. I treat my patio and garden as if they were rooms and place the light accordingly. The play of light and shadows are most dramatic, and illuminations from tiny white lights, flickering candles, or little lamps makes an interesting presentation. Walkways and steps are highlighted for precaution, of course.

A great trick is to have an outdoor chandelier. One can easily be made with a flea-market light fixture that has had the wiring removed. If wind is not a problem, tapers may be inserted where the lightbulbs should go. Use tall votive cups in place of lightbulbs so the evening breeze won't extinguish the flame of the votive candle. Hang the chandelier from an outstretched tree limb over a table for romantic lighting.

Checklist of the Senses
Smell

Mary then took a pound of very costly perfume of pure nard,
and anointed the feet of Jesus and wiped His feet with her hair,
and the house was filled with the fragrance of the perfume.

JOHN 12:3

Smell is perhaps the strongest of our senses. The minute my guests step through my door, I want them to smell something delightful. For instance, my husband loves it when he comes home to a kitchen that smells of pot roast or bread baking. Room sprays, potpourri, pomanders, and candles can make a room smell as wonderful as it looks. Certain fragrances are tied to certain times of the year. Pumpkin bread in the fall and cinnamon-spiced cider for Christmas welcome friends and family to the delights of home.

We become quite accustomed to smells, so unless we deliberately take notice, we're probably not aware of what our homes smell like. Air conditioning and modern-day heating keep them from becoming aired naturally, so mustiness is a distinct possibility. There is nothing like opening your windows and doors to bring in fresh air!

You may not realize it, but our sense of taste is greatly influenced by our sense of smell. When our noses become stopped up and we're sick, food becomes difficult to taste. And our sense of smell becomes even stronger when we are hungry. That's why it's important to use candles that are unscented, such as beeswax, with meals. We want the aroma of the food to be the focus of attention, not the fragrance of the candle. Beeswax candles are odorless, dripless, and have a longer burn time. Making them is labor-intensive, so they're more expensive than regular wax candles. Store all candles in the freezer to make them burn slower and last longer.

A huge, gray, cobblestone fireplace anchors my living room. If I am home during the winter, it usually has a fire in it because I love the way it makes our home smell. Late fall and early winter is a time of year I look forward to because lighting the first fire creates a wonderful atmosphere. The perfume of wood smoke is comforting as it curls up the chimney and chases out the cold. The wood crackles and pops and the flames are so beautiful. A basket by our fireplace holds orange peels and lemon peels. We toss them on the fire periodically for their pleasing fragrance. In the winter I love to let my bread dough rise on a trivet by the hearth. The smell beckons everyone home for dinner.

You can create "scent memories" and set a holiday mood even if you don't have a hearth. For a festive party mood, create the illusion of a cozy

There are two ways of spreading light; To be the candle or the mirror that reflects it.
EDITH WHARTON

fire by gathering and grouping candles. Any mirror adds sparkle to a room, and a strategically placed one in the room can magnify the candle-glow. But remember to never leave a candle unattended.

Any season of the year a pot of coffee perking produces a wonderful smell wafting through the house. And the same goes for the scents of freshly baked apple pie and sugar cookies.

When entertaining in spring, or just for your own enjoyment, notice when gardenias, lilacs, and magnolias bloom. These are some of the most fragrant flowers. Bring them inside to enjoy by the kitchen sink or float them in a crystal bowl on the dining room table.

For fall, sprinkle cinnamon and nutmeg inside a jack-o-lantern. As the candle burns, the spices smell delicious. Scented candles burning create a relaxing mood, making a room warm and inviting while masking household odors.

The fragrance in our bedrooms should be that of tranquility, whereas the fragrance in our kitchen should be that of welcome.

If the world is cold, make it your business to build fires.
HORACE TRAUBEL

Fragrance makes such a personal statement, not only the perfume we wear but also our home fragrance.

The smell of baking bread
is the perfume of comfort.
MASON ELLIS

The fragrance in our rooms is just as important as the colors we choose because we can close our eyes to not see color, but we cannot shut off our sense of smell. Do some research into aromas, and discover what wonderful feelings you can evoke with fragrance. Here are some basics.

There are several ways to provide fragrance for your home. "Essential oils" are derived from a single plant source and are very potent. These oils have perfume, cosmetic, and some medicinal uses. "Fragrance oils" are a blend of synthetic oils and essential oils and intended for fragrance only.

Potpourri is probably the most familiar way to introduce fragrance into your home, but it is just the beginning. First, think of smells that are your favorites. Most smells are floral, citrus, woodsy, or spicy. Add your favorites to your home through potpourri in a bowl and the use of essential oils rubbed on unfinished areas of wood furniture, such

as underneath a table or inside drawers. Oils may damage fine finishes so use them on unfinished areas only. Sachets added to drawers, closets, tucked underneath chair and sofa cushions, or hung over a doorknob add fragrance. A simmering potpourri or essential oil in a pan of water on the stove creates a delightful scent. My favorite secret way to add fragrance to my home is to place a cotton ball with essential oil into the bag of my vacuum cleaner. Lamp rings, porous scented stones, and pomanders are also available.

Flowers every day, all year long, not only look beautiful, but smell wonderful. A bowl of water with a few blossoms floating on top looks at ease in its surroundings and is a natural part of any lifestyle. Placed in the center of the dining room table, it's ready to show-off for company.

Room Fragrance

WINTER

Camellia sasanqua: Camellia blooms come in a variety of colors and can float in a crystal bowl of water to be enjoyed indoors. This plant is a familiar fixture in almost every southern garden because this gem will grow in full sun or partial shade. My horticulture expert and friend, Misty, reminded me that not all varieties are fragrant, so buy one in bloom to be sure.

SPRING

Make a grand European garden for celebrating spring. A silver punchbowl can hold several containers of blooming fragrant spring bulbs…narcissus, hyacinths, pansies, and tulips. Insert each pot into a small Ziplock bag and secure it with a rubber band to keep any excess water from damaging the silver in case it overflows when you water the plants. Use Styrofoam peanuts if you need to bump them up even with the rim of the punchbowl. Tuck in some ivy as filler. Top off the arrangement with a layer of sheet moss. Water often. This type of arrangement looks wonderful and smells fabulous.

Make sure your home smells wonderful. Follow your nose and look for sources of household odors. Vinegar will neutralize most household odors.

The smell of the vinegar will soon dissipate. Baking soda, too, is known for being a deodorizer. Both are natural ingredients and harmless to pets and children.

All Year Long

SUMMER

A shallow pottery bowl that can hold at least one-inch of water can hold several floating, brightly colored zinnia heads. If you don't have these easy-to-grow annuals in your garden or patio, check the local farmers' market for these day brighteners. Plant a gardenia bush just so you can enjoy the fragrant blooms of summer. Mix fragrant herbs, especially rosemary or basil, with your flowers for an extra whiff of fragrance.

FALL

Traditionally, chrysanthemums are the most popular choice for fall. Bring an 8-inch pot indoors and celebrate the season with the vast selection of warm, toasty colors. Find an old enamel saucepan to set the flowerpot inside. If there is extra room, add a few colorful pansies. Fill in any empty space with sheet moss.

My favorite thing to do in the fall is to take a "gathering" walk through our woods. I return with a handful of colorful leaves, berries, and top-heavy grasses.

I bring some indoors and display in a tall, crystal vase. The others make a beautiful arrangement I leave by my back door in an old watering can. For an indoor centerpiece, a hollowed-out pumpkin with a mason jar inside to hold water can display colorful leaves and bright yellow mums. A bit of bittersweet woven into the arrangement or honeysuckle vines curling give added interest. Let a few leaves fall onto the table.

Checklist of the Senses
Hearing

Happiness is like the violin,
it must be practiced.
MR. MCSPADDEN, VIOLIN TEACHER

I am such a believer in background music. When our two sons were beginning elementary school, I researched and found that playing classical music or music written without words helps focus attention. The more I played it, the more their math skills began to improve, and it worked its magic on me, too. The music helped me concentrate on what I was supposed to and drowned out the noises of the other people at home.

The reason for choosing music without words is that it removes the temptation to sing along or drift away in thought. I am not subconsciously thinking, "What's the name of that song?" or "Who sings that?" I am not subconsciously singing along with the words. Classical music has become an integral part of our home, and it still is today. When I arrive home from work, I flip on the stereo and it spills out the comforting "sounds of home." Here are some of my favorites…

1. "Ode to Joy," Ludwig van Beethoven

2. "Sheep May Safely Graze," Johann Sebastian Bach

3. "Brandenburg Concerto #3," Johann Sebastian Bach

4. "Meditation, From Thais," Jules Massenet

5. "Serenade in C," Franz Joseph Haydn

Music is an important part of entertaining, too. Soft, classical music playing in the background encourages conversation by filling the void and quelling uncomfortable quiet moments. Dinner music is one of the best tools for creating a warm atmosphere. Keep the music in the background though, and let your guests' conversations be the predominate stars of the evening.

Themed music can be appropriate for the season. Instrumental Christmas favorites are loaded in my CD player the day after Thanksgiving, and they play right on through Christmas Day. The music sets the tone for the holiday season whether I am hosting a party, decorating the tree, or baking in the kitchen. If there are words in the music, I play it even softer because I want people listening to each other and not singing. Sometimes the music is a symphony orchestra, and sometimes it is country flavored with guitar.

Before your guests arrive, load the CD player with several CDs and hit

There is always music amongst the trees in the garden, But our hearts must be very quiet to hear it.

AUTHOR UNKNOWN

the "repeat all" button. It will be hours before you ever give changing the music a thought.

I am blessed to have two musicians in the family. For special parties, the boys will play their violins as guests arrive, setting the tone for the evening. Guests know they are truly welcomed when played for upon arrival. Having a live musician can be chancy if you are not familiar with his or her playing. If you are hiring musicians to play at a special event, have them play for you before they play for your guests. Also, consider asking young musicians if they will play for your party. Their parents will love it because it gives the children good reason to practice and offers a platform to show their talents.

Each time of the year brings with it sounds of the season. We just have to listen. Summer brings outdoor symphony concerts, including cricket choirs and bullfrog solos. A flag flapping in the breeze on the porch greets all those who enter with the essence of summer. Take notice and listen to the music of God. He has placed around us the whisper of the wind, the patter of the rain, the singing of birds, the crunching of snow, and the most beautiful sound of all—the laughter of children.

Checklist of the Senses
Taste

The prescription for joyful living is very simple:
If you want to be happy, treat people right.
DR. ROBERT SCHULLER

*G*iving your guests something to eat or drink is an immediate offering of hospitality. It doesn't have to be elaborate fare. No person is too small for God's love, and no offering is too insignificant for God's honor. A glass of ice water with a slice of lemon on the rim, a cup of tea, or a soda offered is a thoughtful thing to do. Sometimes your guests will decline, but you have at least extended the invitation. Make this gesture of kindness to guests, to the letter carrier on a hot day, to your son just home from school, or to your husband coming in the door from work. No one can solve all the problems of the world, but we can start with thoughtfulness and kindness.

Food is an essential part of any party. Our happiest celebrations of life's milestones, such as weddings, births, and holidays, are usually centered around the table. Even if you don't enjoy spending a lot of time in the kitchen, there are ways to offer hospitality that include great tastes.

Flavored Iced Teas

Over the years I have collected a cupboard full of clear glass pitchers. Some have been passed down through the years, and some are wonderful flea-market finds. Ice water, tea, or juice looks much more beautiful in a glass pitcher than in a plastic one. Simple iced tea is made more memorable when infused with fresh fruit, such as whole, ripe peaches, crushed strawberries, and pineapple juice or frozen lemonade. Add a vintage iced tea spoon and cloth napkins for a lovely tea tray presentation. It's beautiful, simple, and gracious.

A wise choice is to keep in your pantry several snack options for unexpected company. A tin of shortbread cookies, a jar of nuts, water crackers, and cheese are all simple and take almost no preparation, just a little presentation. A staple in my pantry is a jar of Pecan Pepper Jelly to drizzle over a block of cream cheese and serve with crackers. I keep emergency candles for when the electricity goes out and emergency Pecan Pepper Jelly for unexpected company! I recently served a plate of cubed cheddar cheese and honey mustard sauce to some unexpected guests. Instead of toothpicks, I gathered a few twigs from my garden and inserted them into the cheese for dipping. A cluster of grapes added to the presentation, and it looked beautiful on a silver tray. (Putting almost anything on a silver tray makes it look beautiful and makes your guests feel special.) Their compliments let me know I pleased them.

A WELL-STOCKED PANTRY

For the well-stocked pantry, have several food items available so you don't have to run to the market if unexpected company arrives. By keeping a few things on hand, you can be relaxed and enjoy the arrival of friends. Some basic "Have on Hand" items are:

Nuts

Water crackers

Cheese straws

Pepper jelly

Instant peach tea

Olives and artichokes

Basic cheeses

Bottled water

Canned or frozen juices

Shortbread cookies

Pretty cocktail napkins

Paper doilies

Reunions, homecomings, fund-raisers, and holidays are wonderful opportunities to offer delicious foods. Whether food is eaten with fingers or forks, it's the generous and gracious provision of sustenance that makes an impact during the most difficult of times as well as the good times.

THE UNIVERSAL TREAT— COOKIES

Think back to how many happy memories are tied to the cookie jar. Coming home from school and reaching into the jar. Playing with a childhood tea set and offering cookies on a plate to a gathering of dolls and bears. The box of cookies so carefully packaged and mailed to a soldier in a foreign land as a tangible, treasured comfort of home. To offer authentic, warm-hearted hospitality, a cookie is a quick and convenient taste of home.

One of the things that my sister and I treasure most is Mother's recipe box...or boxes. Our mother made every-thing from scratch, and through the years she collected a huge array of recipes. To our delight, we have the recipes for the cookies she made to go into our childhood lunch boxes: Polka Dot Cookies, Sugar Cookies, and Cowboy Cookies. There is nothing like a plate of freshly baked cookies when guests arrive. Polka Dot Cookies is an easy recipe for sharing. Mother always made a double batch because they never seemed to last very long. Sometimes I make these cookies for my family and pair it with ice cream or fresh fruit. When Polka Dot Cookies are placed in a pretty box and tied with a polka dot ribbon, they also make a memorable gift. Try the delicious Polka Dot Cookies!

POLKA DOT COOKIES

(Makes 1 ½ dozen cookies)

2¼ cups sifted flour
¾ teaspoon baking soda
½ teaspoon salt
1 cup (2 sticks) butter
1 cup firmly packed dark-brown sugar
½ cup granulated sugar

2 eggs
1½ teaspoons vanilla
1 6-ounce package butterscotch flavor
   pieces
1 cup miniature marshmallows

Prepare cookie sheet by lining with parchment paper or a Silpat.

Measure flour, soda, and salt into sifter. In a large bowl, cream butter with both sugars until fluffy. Beat in eggs and vanilla. Sift in flour mixture, ⅓ cup at a time, blending well. Stir in butterscotch pieces.

Drop dough a scant ¼ cup at a time, 6 inches apart on a large, lined cookie sheet. Spread the dough into 4-inch rounds.

Bake at 375 degrees for 10 minutes. Do not over bake. Place several marshmallows on top of each cookie while it is warm. Bake 1 to 2 minutes longer or just until the marshmallows melt. Remove to wire racks to cool.

Cookies lend themselves beautifully to the spirit of hospitality. They are wonderful at special occasions, such as an open house, welcoming a newcomer, or a teacher appreciation tea. For the four o'clock hostess, a few cookies and a pot of tea is really all you need, so the expense is small. And, really, this simple presentation is quite manageable whether for a party of 12 or even 100.

For any special occasion, these Stained Glass Window Cookies require no baking and are a beautiful addition to any table.

STAINED GLASS WINDOW COOKIES
(Makes 3 dozen cookies)

1 12-ounce package semi-sweet chocolate chips
1/2 cup butter
1 6-ounce package colored miniature marshmallows

1/2 cup finely chopped pecans
1 package shredded coconut.

Melt chocolate chips and butter in top of a double boiler and let cool. Add marshmallows and nuts. Form into 2 or 3 logs and roll in coconut on waxed paper. Refrigerate for at least 4 hours. Cut into 1/2-inch slices when ready to serve.

Store thin, crisp cookies in a container with a loose-fitting lid. Store chewy, soft cookies in a container with a tight-fitting lid.

GATHERINGS

Gathering around the table to share a meal is at the heart of hospitality. When people eat together, they show a unity of purpose. We are told Jesus even got into trouble at times because He gathered at what some people saw as "the wrong tables." And, as Christians, we are familiar with gathering at the most sacred table, "The Lord's Supper." Today we still meet at the table to celebrate faith and fellowship. Eating together gives us the opportunity to enjoy friends and family.

Picnics, homecomings, reunions, and tailgate parties usually involve potluck. Potluck means you never know exactly what food will show up at a gathering…your "luck" lies in what comes in guests' pots! And that's what is wonderful!

In the spirit of the old hymn "We Gather Together," our family is no exception. We just celebrated our seventy-third Mason family reunion! The red-and-white plaid, oilcloth-covered tables were laden with new recipes and old family favorites. There were fresh vegetables out of the garden, and someone had even brought a couple of fast food drive-thru containers.

Our clan has grown so much over the years that we hold this "Second Sunday in September" event in a state park pavilion overlooking a beautiful river. Battered work trucks park next to a Lexus convertible and assorted SUVs. Billye and Martha Jane are our official greeters with hugs and open arms. Family members arrive from long and short drives to draw close with food, faith, and fellowship.

A favorite recipe that is good for gatherings is Gazpacho Salad Pasta.

Fresh seasonal food tastes best. Check your local farmers' market for what is in season.

It goes well with chicken, ribs, and ham, and can easily be extended by adding extra cucumbers and tomatoes. Make it the day before, and serve it chilled. It travels well in the car, too. And the leftovers are wonderful! Enjoy them the next day as a salad for lunch.

GAZPACHO SALAD PASTA
(Serves 10-12)

1 16-ounce box Bowtie pasta
1 4-ounce can sliced black olives, drained
½ cup sliced salad olives
6 green onions finely chopped (using both green and white ends)
1 10-ounce can Rotel tomatoes

2 teaspoons garlic salt
3 fresh tomatoes, chopped
1 large cucumber, chopped
1 cup cilantro, chopped
1 8-ounce bottle Ranch dressing
1 8-ounce package shredded cheese (optional)

In a large pot, bring water to boil. Add pasta and cook according to directions on package. Drain immediately and rinse with cold water. Combine pasta with the remaining ingredients except cheese. Mix. Chill overnight to let flavors marry. Just before serving, top with shredded cheese if desired.

Potluck Reminders

- Helium-filled balloons tied out front let attendees know they've reached the right place.

- If the dinner is out of doors, have a Plan B in case of rain.

- Take extra lawn chairs.

- If water is not available at your site, include a bottle of hand sanitizer.

- Set up the food table with plates on one end and the silverware and napkins on the other so you don't have to juggle them in your hands while serving yourself.

- Having drinks on a separate table keeps the food table from becoming congested. And it makes it easier for guests to refill their glasses without fighting a crowd.

- Make sure you have extra everything (food, plates, silverware, game accessories). Someone always forgets something.

- Keep track of what you brought by making a list. Put your name and phone number on your dishes with a piece of masking tape or use an address label.

- If you do not use disposable dishes, use serving dishes that you can afford to get broken or forgotten.

- Slice or scoop food into serving-size pieces before putting them on the table.

- Vintage picnic baskets, dishtowels, and cake takers lend a party atmosphere to the gathering.

For a tailgate tablecloth, keep an eye out for an old stadium blanket. If you find your team's colors, you are the lucky one!

- Tuck in a quilt for young children, teenagers, a husband, or even you for a quick nap!

- Bring plenty of garbage bags so you always leave the site clean. Garbage bags can also surround casserole dishes on car floorboards to prevent stains on carpets.

- Pack some fun: A football to throw or a Frisbee to toss can be great.

- Find some old pictures of people who will be at the party, and bring them along to get the conversation and party started!

- Have everyone sign a guest book, including name, address, phone number, and email address. That way you have a handy list for next year's reminder notices, and you can double-check and update your own address book.

- Even if the date is set a year in advance, designate someone to send out reminders. Include directions and a map. Make sure an RSVP is included so people know how many to plan for.

- Take lots of pictures so they can be enjoyed at later gatherings.

6

Checklist of the Senses
Touch

*There are some people who have the quality of richness and joy in them
and they communicate it to everything they touch. It is first of all a
physical quality; then it is a quality of the spirit.*
THOMAS WOLFE

It feels good to be home." I consider that the best compliment of all! This is what you want friends and family to think when they walk through your door. By keeping the "Checklist of the Senses" in the back of your mind, you can achieve this welcome homeyness.

Touch and texture in a home is so important and can be implemented easily. Indoors, a basket of logs, plump upholstery, a soft throw over the corner of a favorite leather chair…all look inviting.

Living in the country, I use old, galvanized, zinc pails and washtubs when entertaining outdoors. The silver-gray, smooth texture complements the multilayered green grass. And they look so much better than plastic buckets when filled with ice and frosty beverages. These galvanized, country-kind of containers are easy to pick up at flea markets and antique stalls. The tubs come in different sizes, shapes, and conditions. Ones with holes in the bottom are my favorite! They are less expensive, they drain out the water when filled with ice, and if I decide to fill them with flowers later, the drain hole is already there.

For a smooth, cool touch, I fill mason jars with lemon tea ahead of time, add lids, and place in washtubs. Just like soda cans, they are easy to pick up, and the glass jars are cute. The jars can be old, but use new lids, which are readily available at grocery stores.

For a summer outdoor gathering, tie bundles of herbs such as basil, rosemary, and sage to napkins with a bit of raffia or twirling honeysuckle vines. These herbs are in abundance in the summer, and they lend not only fragrance but extra texture as well.

I believe any special gathering will become a more lasting and memorable

> *When people take the time and care to make the presents they give, they put into the gifts not only the materials needed, but also a part of themselves. The thoughts and feelings behind the gift, not the grandness of the gift, are the important ingredients.*
>
> TASHA TUDOR

event if guests are sent home with a special treat, with something they touch. It doesn't have to be a wrapped present or anything expensive that a guest may feel obligated to reciprocate for. Instead, make it a gift of thoughtfulness, such as a few homemade cookies in a cellophane bag, a vintage teacup from the flea market with a packet of herbal tea, or a bottle of flavored vinegar. The sole reason for the gift is to make the recipient feel special and important.

A Gift of Herbal Vinegar

Clean, tall, glass bottle
White vinegar or apple cider vinegar
3 4-inch pieces fresh rosemary

4-6 white garlic cloves
Cork
Colored sealing wax (optional)

Use a pretty, tall bottle you've collected from a garage sale, flea market, or gotten at the store with other ingredients inside. Or you can purchase a bottle at a craft store. A metal lid isn't necessary because you can use corks.

Insert rosemary stems into the clean glass bottle. Drop in garlic cloves. In the microwave or on the stovetop, heat the vinegar until hot but not to boiling. With a funnel, pour the hot vinegar into the bottle with the rosemary and garlic.

Use cork for a lid, and dip into melted wax for sealing. (The wax is not necessary, just a pretty touch of detail.)

A Few Friendship Gifts

- Save small jars. They are the perfect size to fill and tie a ribbon around the neck for party favors. (See the Vanilla Sugar recipe in chapter 8.)

- Round tubes that held potato chips are perfect to stack cookies in. Cover the container in pretty wrapping paper.

- Collect pressed-glass small vases. Fill with herbs from your garden.

Tie on a ribbon and a "thank you for coming" card. Bunch them all together on a silver tray for the party centerpiece. Guests will be surprised that they get to take one home.

- For a garden theme party, at each place setting put a new set of gardening gloves. Tuck in the silverware and tie with a sprig of ivy. Everyone can use a new set of gardening gloves!

- Make herbal votives. Melt left-over candle wax cautiously. Spread dried herbs on a baking sheet. Dip a votive quickly into the melted wax by holding the wick, and then roll it in the crushed, dried herbs. Dip the votive in wax once more to set the herbs. Let them harden on the wax paper. Use a satin ribbon to hold a "thank you for coming "note.

- Lovingly worn teacups and teapots make wonderful containers for planting herbs. Sage, thyme, basil, and rosemary are fragrant gifts from the garden. These are unique gifts!

- Anything you put inside crisp, new cellophane looks special, such as cookies, chocolates, mints, or nuts. Finish with satin ribbon.

- Lily bulbs are perfect gifts for anyone who loves a garden.

> *What you put into the hands of your guests may sincerely touch their hearts more than anything else you do.*
> ALDA

- Unwrap a commercial bar of soap—an herbal soap works wonderfully. To make it look special, wrap it back up in wax paper. Cut ribbon into lengths long enough to wrap around each bar and seal with a sealing wax stamp.

- Vintage handkerchiefs make cute wraps for small gifts. Or use freshly laundered and starched handkerchiefs as napkins at a tea party. Embroider your initial and date of the party on each one for a memorable take-home favor.

- Small silver frames with a picture of each guest or an interesting quote can serve as place-card holders. Guests may take it home as a gift.

- A few words, a poem, or a quote on parchment rolled and tied with a ribbon handed to a guest as she leaves will make her feel special.

The best gift I ever
received was a
"Letter to
My Mother"
from my son during
his senior year
in school. It was
a thank-you gift
that will touch my
heart forever.

ALDA

An
Afternoon
Christmas
Tea

Five Ideas to Make Your Gathering
Delightful

The future belongs to those who believe in the beauty of their dreams.

ELEANOR ROOSEVELT

There really is no great secret to hosting a successful party. Just invite people who are easy to get along with and entertain them graciously. The more you entertain, the more comfortable you will become. Here are some great tips to help you entertain.

1. ESTABLISH A THEME

A party with a purpose is probably the most popular of gatherings. Birthdays, holidays, reunions, and special occasions are all wonderful reasons for a party, but let your guests know exactly what they are invited to. This will help them know how to dress, what to bring, and what to expect. A group of friends just "Catching Up," a "Soup Supper" to break up a cold, long winter, or "Welcome to the Neighborhood" for a new couple in your block are great descriptive titles. Be creative!

Guests will really appreciate knowing the theme...and might even get into the act by wearing costumes or bringing related items or sharing special stories if you invite them to.

2. THE INVITATION:
WHAT, WHO, AND WHEN

The invitation gives the first impression of the party. An engraved invitation or a written invitation is always in good taste. Invitations that are hand-delivered or have elaborate packaging let receivers immediately know they are special. On the other hand, a shout across the backyard fence of "Come over tonight for ham-burgers!" is a welcomed invite. For written and printed invitations, a tagline at the top is good: "Samuel Is Turning 18!" "A Bridal Shower for Amy." "Mason Is Graduating."

Consider the space available to gracefully handle the guests and the arrangements. If I want to invite all 53 teenagers in the church youth group, I will probably hold the party someplace other than my moderately sized living room. If I invite only a committee group of 12, I can handle that with ease at home.

Consider the guest list very seriously. You don't want to forget someone or hurt someone's feelings by not including him or her.

By taking into consideration who is invited, you can plan for the best time of day for the party. My elderly aunt and uncle have given up driving after dark, so family get-togethers are now held on Sunday afternoons. Weekend parties work best for people who work regular jobs. Parties with school-age children are best on weekends

You are cordially invited to an
Afternoon Tea

Date : _____
Time : _____
Place : _____

R.S.V.P.: _____

so homework doesn't interfere. For elementary-age schoolchildren, a party right after school is wonderful and gives them something to look forward to all day. (Children are usually hungry right after school, so food served immediately upon arrival is thoughtful.)

3 . PLANNING AHEAD

By planning ahead, you can be relaxed, and this has a ripple effect on your guests. Thinking through the needs of guests ahead of time eliminates problems, hazards, and embarrassments.

One Christmas we invited elderly neighbors for Christmas dinner. They had no family nearby, so they were thrilled to join us. I knew one woman was in a wheelchair, so my husband and I had to plan how to get her safely inside since we have no wheelchair ramp. Once inside, she would need extra room to maneuver her wheelchair. I placed our furniture a bit differently so she wouldn't feel embarrassed that we had to adjust things for her.

Little thoughtful gestures done ahead of time allow you to interact with your guests and also handle any unexpected issues.

Plan for your guests' arrival and departure. A mirror in the entryway is thoughtful so guests can check their hair and makeup after being out in the weather. Designate a specific place for coats and purses. If the coat closet will not accommodate a large gathering, lay coats and wraps across a bed in a bedroom. This keeps clutter down to a minimum, and guests know immediately where to get their wraps when leaving. And showing guests where to leave or retrieve their coats is a wonderful way to let children be part of the party! If it is raining, offer a place for umbrellas. If you don't own a traditional umbrella stand, a small, plastic wastebasket will serve the purpose nicely. Set this close to the door so water won't be dripped all over your house.

Spread love everywhere you go. First of all in your own house...let no one ever come to your home without leaving better and happier.

MOTHER TERESA

foods you serve on a plate as an artist's palette. There should be an interesting mix of colors. Think baked salmon (pink) garnished with a sprig of yellow lemon slices. Then add green broccoli and orange carrots, and you have a gorgeous and delicious display.

Serve both hot and cold dishes on the buffet table. Even on the hottest of summer days or the coldest of winter days, a medley of hot and cold foods is most pleasant.

If a guest sincerely offers to help, let him or her fill water glasses and do other small tasks. That leaves you free to tend to last minute details.

4. The Food and Drink

Keep refreshments simple. For most dinner parties, choose foods that can be prepared ahead of time—the day before, the morning of, or at least an hour before guests arrive. This way you can enjoy greeting your guests. You'll be under a lot less stress since you've planned wisely. A few well-cooked and thought-out foods that are attractively served are better than a table full of hurried-up foods.

When planning the food menu, think texture. The Chinese are masters of this art, combining chewy foods, such as cashews or fried noodles, with smooth sauces and softer foods. Think about the

5. Adding "Something Extra"

By adding something extra, you have your "Wow!" factor. My goal is to have at least one thing at a party that will generate a "wow" comment. It could be the moss-covered table, the roses center-piece, or the friendship gifts I give to guests as they leave. I hope in some way I have warmed my guests with hospitality and let them know I enjoyed having them at my home. The wow factor does not say, "Look what I can do" or "Look at what I have." It is the crown of hospitality that simply states, "I want to sincerely welcome you, make you feel special, and enjoy your company while expecting nothing in return."

One most memorable "wow" for me were the Sorbet Lemon Cups pre- pared by the hostess and offered after dinner on one of my overseas trips to England. These Lemon Cups were served at a party on a beautiful silver tray. I knew it was something I would always remember and try to replicate at home. They are easy yet so elegant.

RASPBERRY SORBET LEMONS
(Serves 6)

6 lemons, wash and pat dry
Raspberry sorbet or sherbet

Sprigs of fresh mint

Slice the tops off the lemons about one third of the way down and save them for use later. Slice a small sliver off the opposite end of the lemons so they will stand up on the platter or tray. Remove pulp from the lemon shells and save it for lemonade or tea later.

Place the lemon shells in the freezer for at least 2 hours. Remove the sorbet from the freezer, and let it soften. Fill scooped out lemon rinds with sorbet, rounding the top. Place lemon rind tops back on the lemons and gently push them down so they will stay. Put them all back in the freezer to harden until ready to serve. Just before serving, garnish each lemon with a sprig of fresh mint.

A party brings people together and offers the opportunity to witness for Jesus through kindness. People gifted with hospitality can leave an indelible mark in the lives of others whom God brings at just the right time.

8

Entertaining from the *Heart*

What is uttered from the heart alone,
Will win the hearts of others to your own.
JOHANN WOLFGANG VON GOETHE

A tea party is the ultimate form of hospitality. Pairing my love of tea with my love of a garden is a natural. There is such joy in a garden, and so many reasons to entertain there. For one thing, the decorating is already done. God's taken care of that! My garden is an extension of my home. I even have garden rooms. Each "room" offers a different spirit.

Our front porch, with its porch swing dressed with a smooth-to-the-touch quilt, wicker rockers plumped with pillows, a coffee table full of gardening books, delightful bird nests, and myriad plants welcome people to sit for a while. The patio is a bit more formal with ivy topiaries in garden urns. Yet it also has a close, intimate feeling as it overlooks our peaceful lake. Out back we have an outdoor kitchen that hosts teenagers' swim parties and any excuse for a barbecue. (Dining alfresco is a breeze if you can incorporate a grill, small refrigerator, and water faucet in your area layout.)

A WHITE GARDEN TEA

Sipping a cup of tea transports us to a gentler time and place...a time to remember our own self-worth and the joy of friends. It's not what we wear, what we eat, or how fancy the party—it's the warmth of friendship that is to be most treasured. A beautiful, inspiring cup of tea calls for a pause and time to transform the everyday into a rich memorable occasion.

Decorate using white, and plan your menu around white. You can even ask your guests to wear white! Bring out your silver. It will look beautiful with the all-white theme.

For invitations, color-copy seed packets of your favorite white flowers. Insert a few seeds into the envelope so they fall out when opened.

Here are some of my favorite tea-party recipes and take-home favor ideas.

A Friendship Gift of Vanilla Sugar

Vanilla sugar can be used to sweeten anything you would use normal sugar for—pies, puddings, ice creams, cakes, tea, and coffee. It is easy to make, and so delicious to use. Vanilla sugar is perfect for take-home party favors.

Usually this sugar is made using an empty vanilla-bean pod, its seeds having been scraped out for another use. The pod is then put into a jar of sugar, which gradually absorbs the vanilla essence. In this recipe, the strongly flavored seeds themselves are used for quicker results.

Vanilla Sugar

1 vanilla bean, split in two lengthwise
2 pounds sugar

Pressed-glass containers with lids

Scrape seeds of vanilla bean into a bowl and stir in sugar until combined well. Store in an airtight container until ready to use.

Fill glass jars and secure with tape. Tie on a ribbon and hang a pretty tag that has "Vanilla Sugar" written on it, along with some suggested uses.

WHITE GARDEN TEA COOKIES

(Yield about 64 cookies)

1 cup butter

½ cup powdered sugar

1 teaspoon vanilla

2 cups pecans, chopped

2 cups all-purpose flour

6 ounces white chocolate

Cream butter with ½ cup powdered sugar and vanilla until light and fluffy. Add half of the chopped nuts and stir. Blend flour and remaining nuts and add to mix. Shape in balls the size of quarters, and put on parchment-lined cookie sheets. Bake at 325 degrees for 20 minutes. When cool, roll in rest of powdered sugar.

Pulsate the white chocolate in a food processor on coarse. Place the white chocolate in top of a double boiler. Bring the water to boil, and then reduce the heat to low. Melt the chocolate, stirring occasionally. Dip the flat bottom of the cookie into the chocolate and press two cookies together to create little sandwich cookies. Rest them on wire racks until the chocolate has cooled.

Divide the cookies into portions and pack into a medium-size, resealable bag. Wrap the bag in wax paper for a nice gift presentation and place into a decorative white box you can purchase from a bakery supply company. Tie with pretty gold ribbons.

THE BEAUTY OF TEACUP VARIETY

There is such a renewed interest in the art of the tea table. Don't be discouraged from sharing a cup of tea with friends because you don't "have what it takes." You do! If you can boil water, you can make tea. Any teacup will do, and I think it is even more charming when they do *not* match. Sometimes sharing a story of the teacup itself starts a delightful conversation of sharing and remembering.

BUTTON COOKIES
(Makes 2 dozen cookies)

½ of 15-ounce package refrigerated
    piecrusts

¼ cup apricot jam

Preheat oven to 425 degrees.

Unfold piecrust. Press out fold lines. With a 1½-inch round cutter, cut out circles. Place half of the rounds on a baking sheet. (Air baking sheets are my favorite.) Slightly press the remaining rounds with a 1-inch cutter, making an indentation around the rim of the cutout. Cut either two or four holes in the center of the rounds with a straw to resemble buttonholes. Place on baking sheet, and bake for 5 minutes or until slightly brown. Remove to a wire rack and cool. Spread plain rounds with jam and top with remaining "button" rounds.

SAUSAGE PINWHEELS
(Makes 32 pinwheels)

1 pound mild pork sausage
½ cup onions, finely chopped
⅔ cup pineapple preserves
1 tablespoon dry mustard
½ teaspoon salt

¼ teaspoon ground black pepper
⅛ teaspoon rubbed sage
1 package refrigerated piecrusts,
    room temperature

In a large skillet, brown sausage over medium heat. Drain well and add onion. Cook until onion is clear and sausage is well done. Remove the skillet from heat and stir in preserves, dry mustard, salt, pepper, and sage. Cover and chill about an hour.

Preheat oven to 400 degrees.

On a lightly floured surface, use a floured rolling pin to roll one crust into a 12-inch square. Use a pastry wheel to cut dough into 16 3-inch squares. Place these one inch apart on a greased baking sheet. Repeat with the remaining crust. For each pinwheel, use a pastry wheel to make a 1-inch long diagonal cut from each corner. Place a walnut-sized portion of the sausage mixture in the center of each square. Bring *every other* dough tip over the filling to the center of the square. Seal the tips together with water. Bake 9 minutes.

Pineapple Silk

(Makes 8 servings)

This easy, make-ahead Pineapple Silk is delicious and very pretty.

Bottom Layer

¼ cup butter, melted

3 tablespoons sugar

1 cup graham cracker crumbs

Mix the butter, sugar, and graham cracker crumbs well. Divide evenly into 8 stemmed goblets. Press firmly into the bottom of the glasses. Chill in refrigerator for ten minutes.

Middle Layer

½ cup butter, room temperature

1 cup confectioner's sugar

1 egg

In a medium bowl, beat butter, sugar, and egg until the mixture is light and fluffy. Divide evenly into the 8 stemmed glasses.

Top Layer

1 small carton whipped topping

1 20-ounce can crushed pineapple, drained

Fold pineapple into whipped topping. Top each of the 8 stemmed glasses with this mixture. Chill overnight in the refrigerator. Just before serving, place each glass on a doily-lined saucer. As a final touch, garnish with a few extra graham cracker crumbs and a sprig of fresh mint.

SANDWICH LOAF

(Yield: 2 sandwich loaves, about 8 servings each)

This is a beautiful, delicious, and memorable presentation perfect for a White Garden Tea Party!

Prepare the fillings a day ahead of time and chill.

BACON AND EGG FILLING

4 hard-cooked eggs, coarsely chopped
6 slices bacon, cooked to crisp
   and crumbled
1/4 cup mayonnaise

1 tablespoon fresh parsley, chopped
1/4 teaspoon garlic salt
1/8 teaspoon white ground pepper

Place above ingredients into food processor and pulse until well blended. Put in small bowl. Cover and seal with plastic wrap. Store in refrigerator overnight.

CHEESE FILLING

4 ounces cream cheese, softened
1 cup mild cheddar cheese, shredded
1 cup sharp cheddar cheese, shredded
1/4 cup mayonnaise

1 tablespoon pimento, chopped
1 teaspoon Worcestershire sauce
1/8 teaspoon garlic salt

Place these ingredients into food processor and pulse until well blended. Put in small bowl. Cover and seal with plastic wrap. Store in refrigerator overnight.

GREEN OLIVE FILLING

2 3-ounce jars whole, stuffed,
   green salad olives
3/4 cup almonds, slivered
1/2 cup celery, chopped

1/4 cup mayonnaise
2 teaspoons onions, chopped
1/8 teaspoon coarsely ground black
   pepper

Place ingredients into food processor and pulse until well blended. Put in small bowl. Cover and seal with plastic wrap. Store in refrigerator overnight.

SANDWICH LOAVES ASSEMBLY

*2 16-ounce loaves white bread,
    not sliced*

3 8-ounce packages cream cheese

*3 tablespoons ranch style salad
    dressing, prepared*

2 tablespoons butter

1¼ teaspoons prepared mustard

Trim crust from bread so that each side is flat. Slice each loaf *horizontally* into 4 equal layers. Place on a serving plate.

For each sandwich, spread half of each of the fillings between layers of bread. Top the loaf with remaining slice of bread.

In a medium bowl, beat 2½ packages of cream cheese until fluffy. Add salad dressing. Beat until smooth. Spread cream cheese mixture over sandwich loaves and smooth.

In a small bowl, beat the remaining ½ package of cream cheese, butter, and prepared mustard until smooth. Fill a pastry bag with the mustard-cream cheese mixture and put on a small, round tip. Pipe dots onto sides and top of loaves. With a medium ribbon tip, pipe bow and ribbon streamers coming down the sides. With a medium star tip, pipe shell borders around bottom of sandwich loaves.

Place finished loaves in an airtight container and chill at least 2 hours. To serve, cut into ¾-inch slices and place on pretty plates. Decorate the top with fresh white pansy faces or daisy blossoms. If desired, use the blades of green onions for stems.

A Unique Tea Tradition

One tradition of tea is Burnt Sugar. This is simple white sugar turned into a caramel-colored syrup or glittering golden crunchy chunks. Careful attention is required to not let it really burn. It's so simple yet tastes so wonderful!

TEATIME BURNT SUGAR

1 cup of sugar   *Butter, softened*

Line a large cookie sheet with heavy-duty foil. Spread the sugar evenly onto the baking sheet, leaving a 2-inch open border around the edges. With the softened butter, generously cover the border. Place the pan under the broiler. Broil the sugar until it melts. Be careful not to let it burn. When the sugar turns a deep caramel color, remove the pan from the oven. Let it cool. Break the sugar into several pieces. Place in a Ziploc-type bag and pound with a rolling pin to granulate the sugar again. Store in an airtight bag or container because moisture will make it sticky.

Serve Teatime Burnt Sugar in an antique crystal sugar bowl with a pretty silver sugar spoon.

The Art of Being a Guest

Yes, there is an art to being a gracious hostess. But did you know there's an art to being a gracious guest as well? Just as the hostess has certain obligations, the guest has important duties too.

Remember to accept or decline an invitation in a timely manner. If you decline the invitation, it is polite to offer an explanation. You don't have to go into great detail, but be sincere. Once you accept an invitation, stick to your decision even if another invitation arrives.

Arrive at the time noted on the invitation—not early. To be a few minutes late is permissible, and even then you might call the hostess to let her know you are delayed and the reason why.

Be thoughtful when parking your car. Don't entrap anyone's vehicle.

Relax as a guest and try not to be *too* helpful. If a guest is overly helpful, I feel she doesn't think I can handle the occasion.

There is an art to conversation. Just like at a dance, don't be a wall-flower. Try to be entertaining and entertained. Carry on conversations with guests while the hostess is busy. Listen to other guests and show genuine interest in their jokes, opinions, and ideas. You don't have to agree, but don't become testy or argumentative.

Don't outstay your welcome. A rule of thumb for the time to go home from a dinner party is 45 minutes after dessert is served. If the probable end to the party has come and the gathering is still going strong, don't be afraid to be the first one to leave. The hostess will probably be ready for others to follow your lead.

At the door or in the foyer is the place to extend a warm farewell: "Thank you for inviting me" and "The party was wonderful." Don't shout another farewell from the yard or driveway because you might disturb the neighbors.

The next day is a most thought-ful time to phone or even email the hostess and let her know what a nice time you had. For more formal parties, a hand-written, thank-you note of appreciation pleases any hostess.

In Closing

Entertaining can be fun. Don't be afraid to give it a try. Whether it's an elaborate dinner party, a semicasual garden party, or sitting down with friends in your kitchen and having tea, the greatest purpose is to reach out to people—those you know and those you don't know so well.

Be on the lookout for ideas that you can use for your next gathering. Read recipe books, save clippings of centerpieces, watch for teatime books, keep an ear out for great new CDs. Keep the "Checklist of the Senses" in the back of your mind for parties...and also for you and your family's everyday lifestyle.

Hospitality is a gift we give to others and to ourselves. When family and friends gather together, may you enjoy every minute of your time—the anticipation, the preparation, the event, and even the cleanup.

Happy Entertaining!